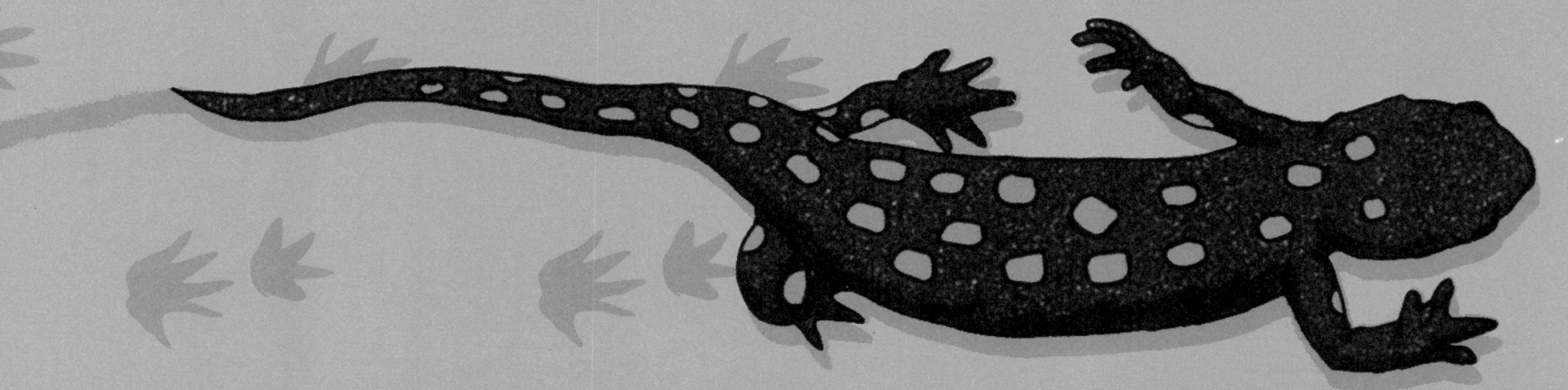

# Salamander Dance

by
David FitzSimmons

Illustrated by
Michael DiGiorgio

WILD IRIS
PUBLISHING

In late winter or early spring, when snow begins to melt and cool rains begin to fall, spotted salamanders crawl out of their woodland hideaways.

They travel at night to vernal pools, shallow depressions that fill with water in spring but often dry up in summer. Vernal pools are perfect places for salamanders to lay their eggs.

Through slippery leaves, down muddy slopes, salamanders slide silently into the rising waters of their vernal pool. They join wood frogs that have also migrated to the pool for egg laying.

All night long, the wood frogs sing.
"Clack! Clack! Clack!"
"Clack! Clack! Clack!"

The water teems with life as insects swim among wood frogs and salamanders. Paying little attention to the other animals, the salamanders gather on the bottom of the pool and begin to dance in the dark.

While the wood frogs sing "Clack! Clack! Clack!," the salamanders twist and turn, swing and sway.

Males move their heads back and forth as they swim around females. With their soft snouts, they gently nudge each other. Following the steps of their ancestors, they dance all night long.

Within three days after their nighttime ballet, females lay eggs, attaching jelly-like sacs to underwater twigs and branches.

Then the adult salamanders slip away into the cool night.

Crawling across the forest floor, they return to their woodland hideaways.

In the vernal pool, the eggs shimmer under the warm spring sun. Inside the eggs, baby salamanders, called larvae, begin to grow.

In about a month, the larvae poke out of their eggs. Surrounding their heads are feather-like gills, which they use to breathe underwater.

The larvae move about the vernal pool, wriggling back and forth. Hungry, they eat all kinds of small animals, including plankton and tiny insects.

The larvae grow bigger and bigger. They flit around with tadpoles and other creatures in the pool.

Spring slips into summer, and the larvae sense that their pool is disappearing. The heat of summer begins to dry up the water. Most or all of it will soon be gone.

The larvae change dramatically now. Their gills start to disappear, and they grow lungs. Their tails grow stouter, and their legs get longer and stronger. This is called metamorphosis.

Then young spotted salamanders leave the nearly dried-up pool and find their own woodland hideaways.

Time passes, and autumn breezes begin to blow.
Fall rains come, and colorful leaves drift downward.

Then snow starts to fall. Nestled in their forest burrows, the salamanders hibernate for the winter.

With the approach of spring, the snow begins to melt and cool rains begin to fall. The vernal pool fills with water again. Wood frogs migrate once again to the wetland and sing.
"Clack! Clack! Clack!"
"Clack! Clack! Clack!"

And spotted salamanders climb from their winter beds and slide silently into the rising waters of their dancing pool.

Once again, the salamanders twist and turn, swing and sway.

All night long they dance and dance and dance.

# Vernal Pools

## TEMPORARY WETLANDS

Vernal pools are shallow wetlands with dramatically changing water levels.

*Vernal pools fill with melting snow and spring rainfall. Sometimes they start to fill in late fall. Unlike most lakes, vernal pools lack a permanent outlet.*

*Vernal pools often dry up in summer. They lose water through seepage into the ground, absorption into tree roots, and evaporation.*

## FORMATION

Vernal pools form in various ways. Glaciers leave depressions in the land. Rivers change courses, their abandoned channels filling periodically with water. Wind erodes sand dunes, producing blowout pools. Gravity pulls down trees, leaving small basins in place of upturned roots. And humans create vernal pools, both unintentionally as by-products of construction and intentionally as restored wildlife habitats.

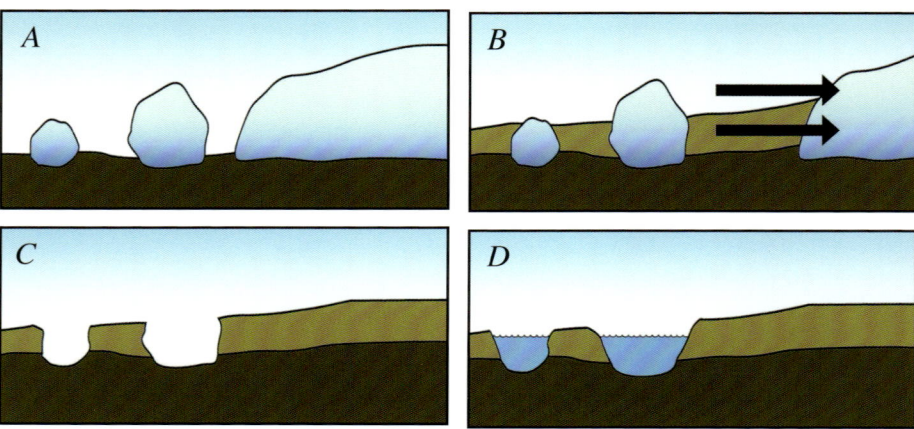

*Glaciers may form vernal pools. Chunks of ice (A) break off the front edge of a retreating glacier. As the glacier melts (B), rocks and sand wash out of the glacier and cover part or all of the chunks. The blocks of ice melt (C), leaving depressions in the land. The rock and sand outwash settles (D), and water fills the small holes, sometimes forming lakes and sometimes vernal pools.*

*Vernal pools may form in ditches and holes dug by humans. Native Americans sometimes created vernal pools when they built earthworks. Today, the construction of beds for highways and railroads may create temporary wetlands.*

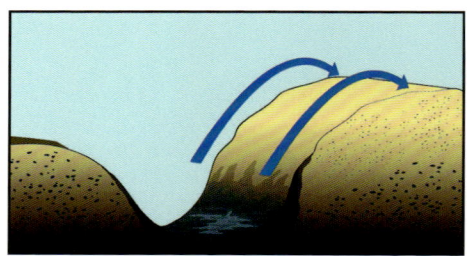

## WILDLIFE

Vernal pools, uninhabitable by fish due to low water levels or complete periodic drying, provide a unique habitat for wildlife. A variety of animals, including amphibians, as well as crustaceans, insects, worms, and other invertebrates, have evolved to migrate to or live in these temporary wetlands, where they may live underwater without the threat of being eaten by fish.

# Spotted Salamanders

## NATURAL HISTORY

Spotted salamanders are mole salamanders. They spend most of the year living in burrows dug by moles, voles, shrews, and other small mammals. Occasionally spotted salamanders move above the surface, hiding under rotting logs or wet leaves.

## MIGRATION

While spotted salamanders remain hidden most of the year, in the spring they migrate to vernal pools on cool, rainy nights. Males arrive first, with females following a few days later. Most return to the same vernal pool in which they hatched.

*During migration to and from vernal pools, salamanders often cross roadways. Concerned citizens often help protect migrating salamanders by putting up warning signs or building amphibian tunnels.*

## DANCING

Spotted salamanders dance as part of courtship. Males swim in circles around females, swinging their heads back and forth across their backs and lifting their snouts under their chins. When a male makes contact, the female touches her head against her partner's body. While dancing, salamanders periodically swim up to the water's surface to breathe.

*After circling around a female, the male leaves spermatophores on the bottom of the pool. The female opens a slit found behind her back legs and picks up the cap of a spermatophore, which then fertilizes her eggs.*

## LIFE CYCLE

Within three days after breeding, females attach egg masses to submerged branches. Each egg mass contains about fifty to one hundred eggs, which hatch in four to seven weeks. Emerging larvae are about one-half inch long. They have small gills and tiny stubs for feet.

*Spotted salamander larvae grow quickly. If they sense rapidly dropping water levels, their bodies develop more quickly. When the larvae reach about two inches, they metamorphose into juveniles and then leave the pool. Like their parents, they descend into burrows or hide under logs and leaves. Juveniles do not migrate back to the vernal pool until they reach adulthood, which takes two to eight years. Spotted salamanders may live to be thirty years old.*

## DIET

Spotted salamander larvae prey upon a wide range of tiny organisms, including daphnia, copepods, isopods, amphipods, and insect larvae. After metamorphosis, they feed in the litter and soil of the forest floor, eating earthworms, slugs, snails, spiders, centipedes, millipedes, and all kinds of insects.

# Glossary

**Amphibian:** a class of cold-blooded animals, such as salamanders and frogs, that typically live in water as larvae and on land as adults.

**Burrow:** an underground hole or tunnel dug by a small animal and used as a shelter or dwelling.

**Evaporation:** the process of changing from a liquid to a gas.

**Gill:** an organ in many aquatic animals used for breathing underwater.

**Habitat:** the environment in which an organism typically lives.

**Hibernation:** a resting state for animals used to survive winter.

**Invertebrate:** an animal lacking a backbone, i.e., a spinal column.

**Larva:** the juvenile stage of life after emergence from an egg and before metamorphosis; plural, larvae.

**Metamorphosis:** for animals, a change in bodily form through growth and restructuring.

**Migrate:** to move temporarily, often seasonally, from one region or climate to another that is more favorable for breeding or feeding.

**Plankton:** small and microscopic organisms that float in water, often a food source for other organisms.

**Vernal Pool:** a temporary wetland filling in late winter or spring and often drying up in the summer, which serves as a fishless breeding habitat.

**Wetland:** a land area saturated with water seasonally or permanently.

*Water Boatman*

*Spotted Salamander*

*For my father, Mick, who encourages my love of nature, especially on nighttime trips to vernal pools.—D.F.*

*In memory of my mentor, Noble Proctor, who was not only a world-renowned naturalist and teacher but also a positive force in encouraging my quest to understand the natural world. Thank you to the superbly talented naturalist, photographer, and writer David FitzSimmons and the master of design, Iain Morris, for having faith in my artistic abilities to bring this book to life.—M.D.*

© 2016 David FitzSimmons. All rights reserved.
Book design by Iain R. Morris.
Edited by Amy Novesky and Donna Linden.

ISBN 9781936607006 (hardcover).
Printed by Great Wall Printing, Hong Kong, China (Job 2059)

FitzSimmons, David. Salamander dance / David FitzSimmons; illustrations by Michael DiGiorgio. pages cm.
 Summary: Explore vernal pools by following the annual life cycle of spotted salamanders, including their springtime migration to these ephemeral wetlands for egg-laying. 1. Vernal pools – Juvenile literature. 2. Spotted salamander – Juvenile literature. 3. Spotted salamander – Life cycles – Juvenile literature. 4. Picture books for children. I. DiGiorgio, Michael, illustrator. II. Title.
QH541.5.P63 F58 2016
2015949118

*Wood Frog*

*Whirligig Beetles*

*Wood Duck (male)*